CONTAINERS BY RAIL IN THE UK

JOHN JACKSON

AMBERLEY

First published 2022

Amberley Publishing
The Hill, Stroud
Gloucestershire, GL5 4EP

www.amberley-books.com

Copyright © John Jackson, 2022

The right of John Jackson to be identified as
the Author of this work has been asserted in
accordance with the Copyrights, Designs and
Patents Act 1988.

ISBN 978 1 3981 0886 8 (print)
ISBN 978 1 3981 0887 5 (ebook)

British Library Cataloguing in Publication Data.
A catalogue record for this book is available from
the British Library.

Typesetting by SJmagic DESIGN SERVICES, India.
Printed in the UK.

Contents

Introduction

Containers are part of our everyday lives, whether stacked in their thousands on a large cargo ship heading for any of the hundreds of container ports around the world, or, individually, on a lorry in front of us on the local motorway.

There are millions of these shipping containers in the world, and their use has played a major part in the globalisation of commerce across the world. Indeed, they are so widespread that there are many examples of their ingenious reuse as a building commodity in themselves. I have seen recent instances of their use as far afield as New Zealand, after the 2011 Christchurch earthquake, and student accommodation in Le Havre in France. Closer to home, another enterprising example is 'Containerville' in East London, a three-storey stack of 40-foot containers, near to London Fields railway station. These adapted shipping container conversions are an East London home to a range of small and start-up businesses.

A recent global estimate of shipping containers in use around the world was around the 20,000,000 mark. Those numbers require a level of standardisation in order for smooth operational handling around the world, using a wide variety of transport methods. For this reason, they are often referred to as intermodal containers, used on ship, road and rail modes of transport. The vast majority of these containers are for general purpose use, usually 20, 40 or 45 feet in length, and either 8 feet 6 inches or 9 feet 6 inches in height. 50-foot containers have started to appear here, with 53-foot containers limited to the USA at present. They are all generally closed containers made of rust-retardant steel. In order to establish an industry standard worldwide, container volumes and capacities are usually referred to as 20-foot equivalent units or TEUs.

The key to the success of these containers lies in the ability to transfer goods between these various transport methods without the need to disturb the container's contents.

So, what part do the railways of this country play in the movement of containers? The story of rail-borne containers begins back in the late 1950s with the introduction of an overnight freight train linking London and Glasgow. These trains were branded 'Condor', derived from 'CONtainers DOoR to door'. As the name suggests, this was a rail freight service introduced in an attempt to compete with the ever-increasing threat of road-hauled transport. The goods were transported in containers mounted on the four-wheeled flat wagons, branded 'conflats', with a full rake consisting of twenty-seven such wagons. A road-based connecting service was offered, I believe by British Road Services, as an add-on service to potential customers within a few miles radius at both ends of the rail operation.

The Condor operated a non-stop service each way between Hendon, in North London, and Gushetfaulds, on the south side of Glasgow. As a young lad, I remember being allowed a late-night pass to see the northbound working on the Midland Main Line as the pair of Metro-Vick Type 2, Class 28, locomotives headed through Northamptonshire. Their use on these services was to be short-lived, as these locos were notoriously unreliable.

The concept of containerised rail freight was established and a second service between Aston, near Birmingham, and Glasgow was added in 1963. These Condor services were to be integrated into a new railway concept introduced two years later. In 1965, primarily as a result of a recommendation included in the infamous Beeching report, the 'freightliner' was born. The containerised rail freight service was extended to movement of goods between approximately fifty depots strategically located around the UK. The more familiar stackable, rectangle container described above was integral to the development of this concept.

In 1968, the Transport Act established a separate commercial company, Freightliner Ltd, wholly owned by the UK government. This company was brought back under British Railways' control some ten years later, as the rail industry sought to carry both 8-foot 6-inch and 9-foot containers. By then, the international opportunities of the UK rail network playing a part in such container movements had been identified. The UK depots underwent pruning with greater emphasis placed in the depots at key British ports. In particular, the close working relations between the railways and the ports of Southampton, Felixstowe and Harwich had been established.

Freightliner's Southampton Maritime and Felixstowe South Terminals, for example, were established in 1972, and have served the industry well for half a century. Back in 2012, the company invested close to £10,000,000 to provide its Maritime terminal with two of the largest rail-served cranes in the UK. This investment coincided with the company's 40th anniversary. This investment also coincided with enhanced rail industry gauge clearances to enable handling of the higher, 9-foot 6-inch, hi-cube containers from the port to the Midlands, north-west England and Scotland.

These fifty years of Freightliner's history have, of course, straddled the mid-1990s privatisation of the rail industry as a whole. Since then, the rail freight sector has seen many significant changes, including the handling of containers by several other freight operators in this privatised era.

Today, three other key players handle rail movement of these containers in the UK, in competition with Freightliner. They are DB Cargo, Direct Rail Services and GB Railfreight.

Taking these three in turn, DB Cargo were known as English, Welsh and Scottish Railways (EWS) around the time of privatisation. At that time, EWS inherited around 1,000 locomotives and approximately 20,000 wagons from the British Rail era. It also controlled around 90 per cent of all rail freight operations. Significantly, though, this did not include container movements in block trainloads. This business opportunity was identified and the company was soon competing for contracts that had historically been in the sole domain of Freightliner. Since 2007, the company has been owned by German railway company Deutsche Bahn and the business rebranded as DB Schenker (and then to DB Cargo).

Direct Rail Services was created by British Nuclear Fuels in the mid-1990s to take over handing of British Rail's nuclear material, which in turn passed into the hands of the Nuclear Decommissioning Authority. This company also diversified from its core business and in 2002 commenced a Grangemouth to Daventry container service for road hauliers the Malcolm Group and the supermarket chain Asda. Significantly, a few years later it was to commence rail movement of containerised goods for Tesco on behalf of Eddie Stobart.

The final major player in today's rail-based UK container operation is GB Railfreight (GBRf). This was a start-up venture post rail privatisation, and, unlike its competitors, was not formed as a result of the division of British Rail assets. Formed in 1999, the company entered the intermodal container market three years later in a joint venture with Mediterranean Shipping Company (MSC). Since then, GBRf have enjoyed sustained growth and a diverse range of wagon types enables them to make a flexible offering to their customers. A more detailed overview of DB Cargo and GB Railfreight is available in two of my earlier publications by Amberley Publishing.

Today, these four operating companies account for the movement by rail of approximately a quarter of all shipping containers arriving in the UK, achieving a 95 per cent reliability measured by trains arriving at their destinations within fifteen minutes of schedule. A wide range of goods are carried ranging from televisions to clothes and whisky to Christmas decorations. This ship to rail traffic, and vice versa, is often referred to as lift-on, lift-off or 'Lo-Lo' traffic.

Less successful has been the rail movement of containers from mainland Europe utilising the Channel Tunnel, with actual traffic volumes consistently falling well below forecasts. A number of external factors have contributed to these reduced levels, including problems with migrants attempting to board tunnel services and UK services being exposed to strike action on the Continent, notably in France.

On a more positive note, Daventry International Rail Freight Terminal (DIRFT) was opened in 1997. At that time, ten trains were operating in and out of the terminal daily, with half of these serving Scottish destinations. It is these longer distance services that logistics companies accept can be operated more profitably, whilst taking a considerable number of lorry journey miles from the UK's congested roads. Daventry's key position in central England, close to motorway links, has led to sustained growth. An extension within DIRFT was completed at the end of 2011. Crucially, the first occupier was the supermarket giant Tesco. Further, a third development is underway as I write these notes.

Some recent improvements within the UK rail infrastructure have benefited container train movements. The completion of the Southampton Freight Train Lengthening Scheme has enabled longer trains to operate at both Millbrook and Maritime terminals in the port. A lengthy passing loop on the Ipswich to Felixstowe branch and a new curve at Ipswich have increased capacity and flexibility at the UK's biggest container port. I have, for a long time, maintained that it is a twenty-first-century embarrassment that a port of such standing should be at the end of a 15-mile-long, partial single-track branch line. Likewise, observation of train movements in Manchester demonstrates the intensity of passenger services through Oxford Road station and Piccadilly's through platforms. Regrettably, that means there are constraints on container services moving in and out of the key intermodal terminal at nearby Trafford Park.

The key to the future success of rail-borne container traffic will be in the rail industry's ability to consistently deliver the reliable service that freight customers demand. These rail movements are but one transport element in the customer's overall supply chain. Shipping companies can, for example, switch between UK ports often at short notice demanding the rail industry responds.

In this publication, we take a detailed look at this container traffic, the key players, the rail workings and the rolling stock used. I hope that you enjoy browsing the pages as much as I have enjoyed compiling them.

In concluding this introduction, and at a time when carbon emissions and climate change are firmly in the global spotlight, it is perhaps appropriate to leave the last word to an industry employee. Earlier this year a Freightliner driver in the cab of her Class 90 locomotive heading through the Scottish Borders commented 'You're going alongside the M74 motorway at times, looking at the lorry drivers and feeling quite smug'. She marvelled at the fact that her freight train could carry seventy-six times as much cargo as a single HGV.

John Jackson

British Rail and Freightliner

For more than a quarter of a century, British Rail moved shipping containers between UK docks and a number of inland terminals. In a typical scene, Brush Type 4 locomotive No. 47309 passed Basingstoke on 5 October 1991 hauling a container working to Southampton Docks. On rail privatisation in the mid-1990s these Freightliner services were to be operated by a management buyout team, retaining the 'Freightliner' branding.

An early example of British Rail Freightliner stock is seen outside the National Railway Museum, York, in November 2015. This flat wagon, numbered 601652, was built in 1971 at BR Ashford. It is seen carrying a guard's caboose, number 99Z04 (09Z04 wrongly applied). These cabooses were used in the mid-1960s as guard's compartments but regarded as an uncomfortable ride for its occupant and were quickly phased out.

Twenty years later in 1990, Freightliner placed a substantial order for a total of 700 wagons, designated FSA (outers numbered 608001 to 608560)) and FTA (inners numbered 607001 to 607140). They were manufactured by French company, Arbel Fauvet. The entire order was delivered by the end of 1993 and was to be the mainstay of the container fleet when Freightliner passed into private ownership soon after. In January 2017, pioneer FTA 607001 is seen passing through Leicester.

After using Class 47 diesel locos and their Class 57 variants for several years, Freightliner turned to General Motors' Class 66 diesels with pioneer No. 66501 *Japan 2001* being delivered in July 1999. On 24 March 2016, it is seen heading through Peterborough on a container train from Doncaster to Felixstowe.

These Class 66 locomotives have worked most of Freightliner's container services during the last twenty years. On 9 May 2017, No. 66418 *Patriot – In Memory of Fallen Railway Employees* heads north through Leamington Spa on a working from Southampton to Garston, on Merseyside.

A network of Freightliner services operates to and from the major container ports of Southampton, Felixstowe and, more recently, London Gateway. In September 2020, No. 66546 is working to the London port. It has just left the Birmingham container terminal at Lawley Street and is passing Water Orton in the Birmingham suburbs.

Freightliner's rail-borne container movement has to compete with road transport. It is generally regarded to have a competitive advantage on journeys over 150 miles, rather than on shorter journeys. In September 2019, No. 66511 heads westwards through Melton Mowbray on a Felixstowe to Crewe working. This routing via Peterborough, Leicester and Nuneaton covers a distance of 227 rail miles.

Freightliner's chief destination in South Wales is Wentloog, on the outskirts of Cardiff. On 16 September 2019, No. 66541 is seen passing eastbound through Newport on a return working from there to Felixstowe. The train is a few minutes into its scheduled eight-hour journey to the Suffolk port.

On 11 July 2019, the same Wentloog to Felixstowe working is seen with No. 66590 in charge. The loco is awaiting departure after a signal check alongside Acton Yard, in West London. The working will now cross London via the congested North London line before reaching the Great Eastern Main Line at Stratford.

Freightliner services from Felixstowe join the main line at Ipswich. On 29 September 2016, No. 66550 hauls a fully loaded service through Ipswich station. Its destination is the Birmingham terminal at Lawley Street. This working will also be routed via the North London Line and then join the West Coast Main Line at Willesden Junction.

Another westbound liner from Felixstowe is seen passing through Ipswich on 2 May 2019. This is the view from the station footbridge as No. 66524 takes the centre road as it joins the Great Eastern Main Line heading towards London.

The port of Felixstowe is the UK's largest container port, handling around half of all of Britain's container traffic. It is rail served via two terminals, north and south. The station at Frimley, on the Ipswich to Felixstowe branch, witnesses all freight services to both terminals, with the lines to the two terminals splitting at the end of the station platform. On 8 September 2017, No. 66526 is seen passing with a Felixstowe North Terminal to Crewe service.

Sister locomotive No. 66548 has taken the same route from Felixstowe to the London suburbs and has just joined the West Coast Main Line (WCML) to head north. It is passing through Harrow and Wealdstone on 15 July 2021 on a working to Lawley Street, Birmingham.

Most of Freightliner's WCML services from Felixstowe to the West Midlands and north-west England travel via the Northampton loop then northwards to Nuneaton. The services destined for the Liverpool and Manchester area then continue along the Trent Valley. On 14 March 2017, No. 66569 is seen passing through the platform at Tamworth on a service to Ditton on Merseyside.

The route via the London suburbs allows Freightliner to opt for electric traction on some services to and from Ipswich. A loco change is then necessary for a diesel to take the train on the non-electrified branch to the Port of Felixstowe. The ageing Class 86 electric locos, dating back to the 1960s, have, until recently, seen use on these services. Pairings such as Nos 86608 and 86622, seen here on 8 May 2017, proved extremely popular with rail enthusiasts. The veterans are heading south through Tamworth on a service from Trafford Park, Manchester, to Felixstowe.

A number of Freightliner's longer distance services are scheduled to layover in their yards at Basford Hall in Crewe, enabling a change of locos if required. On 21 April 2016, Nos 86613 and 86614 pass through Bletchley on an Ipswich to Crewe working.

Heading in the opposite direction on 29 September 2017 are Nos 86607 and 86622, powering south through Bletchley bound for Ipswich. As already mentioned, both these trains require a switch to diesel power between Ipswich and Felixstowe.

Freightliner services to and from Felixstowe also serve several terminals on the eastern side of England, including Teesside. The company switched its services from Wilton to P D Ports' expanded terminal at Teesport in 2014. On 18 April 2018, No. 66537 waits at Grangetown Junction to commence its journey from Teesport to Felixstowe.

The previous day's working, hauled by No. 66571, is seen on the northern approaches to York. It has reached the East Coast Main Line (ECML) at Northallerton and will travel south-eastwards across East Anglia once it reaches Peterborough. The total distance using the ECML is around 270 miles.

The Freightliner terminal at Stourton, Leeds, is regularly served by workings to and from Felixstowe, via Peterborough. Most container trains are operated between Doncaster and Peterborough, via Gainsborough and Lincoln. This eases the increasing passenger timetable pressure on the 80-mile stretch of the ECML between these two important junctions. On 29 January 2019, Nos 66550 and 66501 pass through Gainsborough's Lea Road station heading towards Lincoln on a service from Leeds to Felixstowe.

The terminal at Stourton is seen here on 23 May 2021, in a photo taken from the nearby Freightliner loco maintenance facility at Balm Road. Their loco, No. 66533, is awaiting its next duty with an impressive array of containers all around.

The Stourton site has been used for container traffic since 1967. Today, a service between Stourton and London Gateway offers a rare chance of a container working on the southern stretch of the ECML south of Peterborough. On 5 August 2020, No. 66550 assists No. 66951 on a southbound working seen passing Tempsford crossing, north of Sandy. The train had spent several hours in the loop at Conington earlier. It will now reach London Gateway via Finsbury Park and Stratford in the London suburbs.

By the time this photo was taken, on 7 August 2019, Freightliner had passed into the new ownership of Genesee & Wyoming Inc. This US company owns or leases over 100 railroad companies worldwide. Their corporate branding has been applied to a few locos in their UK Freightliner fleet, including No. 66415. It is seen here passing Chesterfield on a working from Leeds to Southampton.

Another Southampton-bound Freightliner service is seen passing Tamworth in March 2015. Class 66 locomotive No. 66420 is hauling a working from Garston, Merseyside. The loco was originally operated by Direct Rail Services (DRS) and subsequently acquired by Freightliner in 2011. It still retained DRS's corporate colours when this photo was taken.

Three years later, on 5 April 2018, No. 66529 is seen heading in the opposite direction on a Southampton to Garston working. The train is about to leave Acton, West London, and make the short journey round north London to Wembley Yard. It will later continue on the WCML towards Merseyside.

Freightliner has a choice of several routes for operating its container services to and from Southampton. On 13 September 2021, No. 70002 approaches Nuneaton on a Lawley Street, Birmingham, to Southampton working. It will reach the south coast port via Coventry, Leamington Spa, Reading and Basingstoke.

On 6 May 2021, sister locomotive No. 70001 heads a Southampton to Lawley Street working through Kings Sutton station, near Banbury. This train will operate via Solihull, rather than Coventry. It will then reverse into the Birmingham terminal using Washwood Heath goods loop.

These General Electric Class 70 diesel locomotives supplement the Freightliner Class 66s on this container traffic, with a pool of nineteen locos available. On 28 June 2017, No. 70007 heads south through Stafford on a Trafford Park to Southampton working.

On 23 June 2016, No. 70010 is also heading to Southampton seen passing through Bletchley on the WCML. This train is a service from Daventry International Rail Freight Terminal (DIRFT). This rail and road transport hub in Northamptonshire plays an important role in container movements around the UK. It is conveniently situated close to several key roads, namely M1, M6, A14 and A5. Its rail connection is via a spur from the Northampton loop, about 4 miles east of Rugby.

Freightliner faces strong competition amongst the UK rail freight operators. This is particularly true in the case of the Anglo-Scottish market. For several years, Freightliner operated services between DIRFT and Coatbridge in Central Scotland. On 19 May 2017, a pair of Freightliner's Class 90 electric locomotives, Nos 90048 and 90043, head north through Nuneaton on a service to Coatbridge.

Another Class 90 pairing are heading in the opposite direction on 18 October 2018. On this occasion No. 90048 is paired with sister loco No. 90042, as they head through Tamworth with around 30 miles to go on a service to DIRFT.

Two weeks later, and at the opposite end of the UK, No. 66547 is seen close to journey's end as it passes through Whifflet, in the Coatbridge suburbs, on 8 November with a northbound working from Daventry to Coatbridge Freightliner Terminal. The Coatbridge terminal has notched up over half a century of use, surviving when others have been pruned from the Scottish network.

These Anglo-Scottish Freightliner services are all routed on the West Coast Main Line via Carlisle and Crewe. On the evening of 22 October 2021, Nos 90042 and 90047, the latter in the latest Genesee & Wyoming livery, pause for a crew change in Carlisle on a Coatbridge to Crewe service.

There have been few Freightliner workings from the east of London to the west of England. The terminal at Bristol, west of Temple Meads station, closed in 2019, with remaining traffic being transferred to Wentloog, in South Wales. On 6 June that year, No. 66572 approaches Temple Meads on a service from Felixstowe to the terminal.

South Wales has faired a little better. On 22 February 2018, No. 66529 passes through Cardiff Central on a service from Tilbury to Associated British Ports terminal at Barry Docks.

The scale of Freightliner's UK container operation is evidenced in this scene on the dockside at Southampton. The company runs over 100 services each day from the ports of Southampton, Felixstowe, and London Gateway. It is estimated they moved around 770,000 containers by rail in 2021.

In 2012, Freightliner unveiled its investment in two new cranes for its Southampton operation. Coinciding with the 40th anniversary of operations, the cranes were named Freightliner Fortis 15-10-2012 and Freightliner Agilitas 15-10-2012. Fortis represented strength and power, whilst Agilitas represented ease of movement and efficiency.

The extensive loading facilities at Southampton Maritime terminal are evident in this view on 21 March 2019. The main line on the left leads to Southampton, Eastleigh and the north.

Southampton's second Freightliner facility is at nearby Millbrook. On Sunday 27 June 2021, the terminal has No. 66515 in residence, stabling for the weekend.

DB Cargo

Rival freight operator, English, Welsh & Scottish Railways (EWS), was created at the time of rail privatisation in the mid-1990s. After several rebrands, it is known as DB Cargo today. EWS started competing for intermodal contracts almost immediately after privatisation. One of their earliest services linked the Manchester terminal at Trafford Park with Southampton. On 5 May 2016, No. 66175 passes Tamworth on a southbound working.

Almost exactly a year later, in May 2017, it is the turn of No. 66030 to haul the same working. On this occasion the fully loaded working is seen passing through Leamington Spa station.

This final photo of the same working was taken in November 2021 as the train halted for a crew change in the station platform at Nuneaton. A glance at the wagons' paperwork showed a random snapshot of three consecutive containers destined for such diverse countries as Australia, South Korea and Delaware in the USA.

DB Cargo intermodals from Trafford Park also serve the port of London Gateway. On 18 April 2016, No. 66199 heads south through Nuneaton on the West Coast Main Line (WCML). The front of this well-loaded train is monopolised by containers owned by German container giant Hamburg Sud.

Another Trafford Park to London Gateway service is seen heading south through Stafford on 28 June 2017 with No. 66160 in charge. The DP World logistics hub at London Gateway offers berths for up to three of the world's largest container ships simultaneously and claims to be the UK's largest port rail terminal.

Another regular DB Cargo intermodal service links the port of Southampton with the Midlands rail terminal at Birch Coppice, near Tamworth. On 31 January 2020, No. 66185 passes Kings Sutton, near Banbury, on this working.

The same working is seen on 18 May 2021, this time just 7 miles from its journey's end. On that day, No. 66140 is in charge as it passes Water Orton, on the outskirts of Birmingham. The train will take a short branch line off the Birmingham to Derby line at nearby Kingsbury. The business park at Birch Coppice is on the site of a disused colliery.

Another inland terminal served by DB Cargo is Wakefield Europort, in West Yorkshire. It is situated 3 miles to the north-east of Wakefield city and it, too, is built on a former colliery. It was originally opened, in 1996, in anticipation of rail-borne freight traffic generated by the Channel Tunnel opening. On 22 March 2017, No. 66027 is seen preparing to leave the terminal.

One of the regular DB Cargo services to and from West Yorkshire is seen on 2 May 2019. No. 66047 is passing Stowmarket signal box as it heads an intermodal from Wakefield Europort to Felixstowe.

A little later on its journey, No. 66047 is seen again using the recently constructed Bacon Curve in Ipswich. This improvement has enabled all freight operators increased flexibility in the routing of services in the Ipswich area, enabling trains from the north avoiding reversal in the yard there.

DB Cargo also operate services to and from the logistics park at East Midlands Gateway. Located near to Castle Donington, and close to the M1, the terminal opened to rail traffic in 2019. In January 2020, No. 66175 is seen at Marholm, north of Peterborough, and is about to head westwards on a service from Felixstowe to the newly opened terminal.

On 12 April 2016, No. 66151 heads through the high-level platforms at Tamworth. It is on a working from Felixstowe to the nearby intermodal terminal at Burton-on-Trent.

On 16 July 2015, No. 66115 approaches Cardiff Central station on a DB Cargo feeder service with containers to Associated British Ports at Barry Docks. This is one of the few container services operated by DB Cargo in Wales.

Container traffic via the Channel Tunnel has consistently failed to meet the forecasted volumes. Many reasons are offered, including the ongoing issues with migrants attempting to use the tunnel to reach the UK as well as the differences in rail gauges in use, and train lengths permitted, across mainland Europe. One such working from Trafford Park to Bari, in Italy, is seen at Rugby on 18 November 2015. The train loco, No. 92038, had earlier encountered problems and had been rescued by No. 57313.

DB Cargo also has a share of intermodal traffic in the important Anglo-Scottish market. On 23 May 2016, No. 66103 passes Rugby on a service from Scotland's leading container port of Grangemouth to Daventry International Rail Freight Terminal (DIRFT) in Northamptonshire.

On 7 November 2018, No. 66130 is bound for Grangemouth when passing through Whifflet on a service from Mossend Yard, near Glasgow. The Grangemouth complex is conveniently located in central Scotland, halfway between Edinburgh and Glasgow.

DB Cargo have a small pool of Class 90 electric locomotives. These locos work in pairs on Anglo-Scottish services that include the challenging inclines of Shap, in Cumbria, and Beattock, just across the Scottish border. On 24 March 2017, Nos 90034 and 90037 head south through Stafford on a service to Daventry.

On 8 May 2017, another pairing, Nos 90028 and 90036, are in charge of this Mossend to Daventry working. They are seen passing Tamworth using the Up fast line here.

Direct Rail Services

Freight train operator Direct Rail Services was created by British Nuclear Fuels to specifically handle nuclear material rail movements on the privatisation of British Rail. By 2002, the company had also entered the intermodal marketplace, with services between Scotland and Daventry International Rail Freight Terminal (DIRFT). On 17 June 2015, No. 66433 heads north through Nuneaton on a service from DIRFT to Coatbridge.

Direct Rail Services (DRS) also link the terminal at Daventry to the deep-sea wharfs of Tilbury and Purfleet on the north bank of the Thames. This working is operated on behalf of logistics company J. G. Russell. On 21 April 2017, No. 66305 takes the curve through Long Buckby station shortly after leaving DIRFT on its journey to Purfleet.

A year later, on 5 April 2018, No. 66430 is seen on the same working, this time passing through Harrow and Wealdstone in the North London suburbs. The train will shortly leave the West Coast Main Line at Willesden to reach Purfleet via Gospel Oak and Barking.

Since 2012, DRS has also operated a daily service each way between DIRFT and the terminal at Wentloog in South Wales. On a cold day in December 2017, No. 66304 heads through Nuneaton on the service bound for South Wales.

In partnership with Stobart Rail, DRS operate the service on behalf of Tesco. Tesco goods are moved to the company's distribution centre at Magor, close to the Cardiff Wentloog site, for onward local movement by road. On 24 August 2021, No. 66433 approaches Water Orton, on the outskirts of Birmingham, heading for Wentloog.

In 2019, DRS commenced operating a service between Tees Dock and Daventry. This Tesco working is seen on 18 February 2020 as it approaches Burton-on-Trent hauled by No. 66428.

In 2017, DRS took delivery of a fleet of ten Class 88 electro-diesel locomotives. These have become regular performers on the Anglo-Scottish intermodal services. On 2 October 2017, No. 88009 passes Oubeck loops, south of Lancaster, with a Daventry to Mossend working.

On 9 July 2021, No. 88005 is seen heading in the opposite direction as it passes Nuneaton, heading for Daventry. These services have been operated continuously by DRS since 2006, except for a brief period in 2010 when DB Cargo provided the haulage.

This Tesco service has expanded since its introduction and now transports thirty-four Tesco containers at a time, operating six days per week. In November 2018, No. 88008 heads through Lockerbie, in the Scottish Borders, with a service to Mossend.

These Daventry to Mossend intermodal workings are scheduled to complete their journey in just under eight hours. This includes a layover of around an hour at Carlisle. On 20 July 2019, No. 88010 has just recommenced its journey north from there and is about to rejoin the West Coast Main Line at Floriston, close to the Scottish border.

By way of contrast, a pair of DRS's Class 68 diesel locomotives was in charge of this working at Carlisle on 23 October 2021. No. 68018 leads sister loco, No. 68006, as they wait at a signal stop in the station before heading north to Mossend.

The persistent efforts of pioneers such as J. G. Russell, Stobart Rail and W. H. Malcolm has seen container traffic being rail hauled to Central Scotland and beyond. For example, a regular daily Tesco service now operates between Mossend and Inverness. On 2 April 2015, DRS Class 66 loco No. 66427 heads south through Pitlochry on the return working from Inverness.

The Inverness service runs the length of the Highland Main Line to Perth, much of which remains a single-track railway. This often results in freight trains being held in favour of passing passenger services. On 9 October 2017, No. 66423 has reached the loop at Carrbridge station, before entering another single-track section as it heads south.

A little further north at Tomatin, No. 66301 is seen on 25 October 2021 with the southbound Tesco service. The 'Tesco' and 'Less Co' branding on the wagon sides is proudly displayed as the train crosses the viaduct. The length of passing loops on this line restrict the train to twenty containers, well below the loco's capability. The constraints of a single-track railway with short passing loops seem unjust considering the vast sums of money being spent on the A9 Inverness to Perth trunk road scheme.

Scotland's largest port, Grangemouth, has recently benefited from the completion of much-improved facilities at its freight hub, including the capacity to handle longer trains. A regular intermodal service operates from there to Aberdeen. On Saturday 7 October 2017, No. 66424 passes Gleneagles as it heads for Aberdeen.

This well-established DRS intermodal service brings a rare regular freight service to Eastern Scotland, conveying goods for both Asda and Tesco. On 25 October 2018, No. 66423 is seen close to Stonehaven as it nears the end of its journey.

GB Railfreight

Founded in 1999, GB Railfreight (GBRf) entered the intermodal marketplace in 2002 launching a service for Mediterranean Shipping Company (MSC) from the Port of Felixstowe. On 7 September 2017, No. 66770 is seen at Westerfield, on the Felixstowe branch, at the start of its journey to the freight terminal at Hams Hall in the West Midlands.

Hams Hall is owned by Associated British Ports (ABP) and is located close to the Nuneaton to Birmingham line, near to Coleshill Parkway station. On 5 October 2020, No. 66736 passes Cheddington on a service to Hams Hall routed from Felixstowe via both the Great Eastern and West Coast Main lines.

GBRf uses two route options on these services, with the second option to travel across East Anglia via Ipswich, Peterborough and Leicester. On 14 September 2016, No. 66748 is seen passing Marholm, to the north of Peterborough. It will shortly pass through the city's station and head eastwards towards Ely and Ipswich in order to reach Felixstowe.

On Saturday 16 December 2017, No. 66742 is also working cross-country to Hams Hall from Felixstowe. It, too, is seen at Marholm, north of Peterborough. It will shortly head westwards towards Leicester and Nuneaton then onwards to Hams Hall.

GBRf has steadily increased its intermodal services since that inaugural service to Hams Hall. This includes a service to the terminal at Birch Coppice, near Tamworth, a few miles to the north-east of Hams Hall. Commencing in January 2019, this service has taken the cross-country route via Peterborough from the outset. On 14 July 2021, No. 66781 hauls a returning service to Felixstowe through Oakham.

On the afternoon of 29 July 2021, No. 66785 heads west through Hinckley, Leicestershire, working to the Birch Coppice terminal.

One of GBRf's earliest intermodal services operated to Selby, North Yorkshire, on behalf of MSC. Potter Logistics, Selby's owners, recognised the rail potential, increasing the length of its headshunt in 2014 to enable train lengths up to 775 metres. On 3 February 2016, No. 66743 heads through Doncaster on the southbound working from Selby to Felixstowe.

More recently, GBRf operate two services daily between another Yorkshire terminal at Masborough to the Port of Felixstowe. On 8 March 2018, No. 66724 passes Gainsborough Lea Road on one of these services to Felixstowe. This route via Lincoln sees an increasing volume of freight traffic pathed to avoid using the East Coast Main Line between Doncaster and Peterborough.

GBRf operates a daily service linking Trafford Park, Manchester, with Felixstowe. In common with other operators, their services have to negotiate the busy through platforms at Manchester's Piccadilly station in order to access the freight terminal. On 9 September 2021, No. 66711 snakes through Piccadilly's platform 13 on its journey south.

In November 2017, GBRf commenced its first service out of Southampton. Working with logistics company Wincanton it operates a West Midlands service to Hams Hall and, as in the case here, to Birch Coppice. On 6 May 2021, No. 66703 heads south through Kings Sutton on the return working to Southampton.

GBRf also operate a regular service between Southampton Western Docks and Doncaster Inland port (Iport). On 2 September 2021, No. 66711 heads north on the Doncaster-bound working. The location is Toton Yard, an area steeped in railway freight history but less known for passing intermodal traffic.

The DP World deep-sea container terminal at London Gateway opened in 2013. It now sees GBRf operating a number of daily intermodal trains on a variety of routes. On 29 April 2019, No. 66773 passes Milton Keynes Central on a service to Hams Hall.

Evidence of GBRf's continued expansion is seen in these two more recent additions to its services. First, in 2019, No. 66789 approaches Doncaster on a Tees Dock to Doncaster Iport service, operated by GBRf on behalf of IKEA.

Secondly, in November 2020, GBRf announced a new intermodal flow between East Midlands Gateway and the Port of Liverpool. In partnership with MSC, GBRf is providing rail rather than road transport for the land leg of the journey from Seaforth Docks, for the 100 miles to East Midlands Gateway. On 6 August 2021, No. 66781 hauls the Liverpool-bound service through Stafford.

The postponement of the proposed double tracking of the cross-country route to the south-east of Ely means one of the bottlenecks for GBRf remains. On 1 September 2017, No. 66709 passes Barway crossing, on the single line stretch between Ely and Soham, with a Felixstowe to Birch Coppice service.

Freightliner's No. 66567, with No. 66534 for company, has had to wait for the GBRf working to reach Ely before continuing its own journey in the opposite direction. The pair are on a Lawley Street, Birmingham, to Felixstowe service as they, too, pass Barway in the single-track section.

Container trains meet at Manea in May 2020, with Freightliner's No. 66953 about to pass GB Railfreight's No. 66735. The environmental benefits are clear when you consider the combined loads are the equivalent of over a hundred HGVs removed from East Anglia's roads.

UK Supermarkets and Logistics Companies

Back in the late 1990s the supermarket chain Safeway was delivering goods to Millburn Yard, Inverness, for onward movement to their stores in the area. Their shops in Inverness, Nairn, Elgin and Buckie were serviced from there. The rail service was provided by DB Cargo (then EWS). In this June 1999 view, DB Cargo's Nos 66060 and 66119 stand alongside a Safeway container in the yard.

Inverness's Millburn Yard remains in use today, although Safeway was acquired by Morrisons back in 2004, and that rail traffic ceased. On 12 October 2021, Tesco's use of rail delivery is evident by these branded containers stacked high in the yard.

Asda also use Anglo-Scottish services for movement of their goods. One of their branded containers is seen at Carlisle in October 2021. It is in the consist of DB Cargo's service from Daventry to Grangemouth.

Sainsbury's uses rail for container movements between England and Scotland. In a partnership with logistic services company J. G. Russell, goods are transported on DRS workings between Daventry and Mossend. One of their branded containers is seen passing Carlisle in October 2021.

Stobart Rail have been using DRS services to move goods, chiefly for Tesco, between Daventry and Scotland since 2006. One of their containers is seen at Carlisle, branded 'Working Together We Deliver a Greener World'. The company has recently been sold to a German company, Bavaria Industries Group. The future of this rail-borne container traffic is uncertain at present.

Logistics company W. H. Malcolm is a well-established player in container movement in the UK. The family-run business was started around 100 years ago, using a single horse and cart for collection, bagging and delivery of coal from their local railway station. Today the company has over twenty years' experience in rail freight. One of its branded containers is seen at Carlisle in October 2021, in a working from Tees Dock to Mossend.

Global Shipping Container Operators

The latest figures from 2019 suggest that one in four of all sea containers arriving in the UK are moved inland by rail. Each intermodal freight train removes up to seventy HGVs from Britain's roads. From televisions to clothing, from bottled water to whisky and even Christmas decorations, the list of goods transported across our rail network is virtually endless. Freightliner's No. 70006 and GBRf's No. 66712 pass each other at Nuneaton on 5 July 2021.

This photo of Southampton Maritime rail terminal in June 2021 shows the variety of companies whose containers pass through this rail hub. In this section we take a detailed look at the biggest names in container shipping.

The world leader in container shipping is A. P. Moller – Maersk, usually shortened to Maersk. The Danish shipping giant, founded in 1904, has been the largest shipping container operator since 1996. Amongst recent acquisitions, Hamburg Sud, the German shipping company, was purchased in 2017. Cargo ship container capacity is universally measured in Twenty Foot Equivalent Units (TEUs) with Maersk topping the latest listings with just over 4.2 million as of October 2021. Two Maersk 40-foot dry containers, each equivalent to 2 TEUs, are seen in a Freightliner service bound for Felixstowe.

Hamburg Sud branded containers are still commonplace across the rail network. This container is heading to the West Midlands terminal at Hams Hall within a GBRf intermodal from Felixstowe.

In common with other shipping companies, Maersk offers their customers the option of block train (between forty and fifty containers) or single full container load (FCL) shipping. Their containers dominate this GBRf working to the West Midlands.

Mediterranean Shipping Company (MSC) are ranked a close second in terms of capacity with just under 4.2 million TEUs. The Geneva-based company has worked in partnership with GBRf in the UK since 2002. In May 2021, the two companies agreed a five-year extension to their joint operations. A GBRf working is seen at Leicester with a 20-foot and a 40-foot MSC container maximising the space on the GBRf flat wagon.

The third ranking shipping operator is Compagnie Maritime d'Affretement (CMA) & Compagnie Generale Maritime (CGM). This French operator, based in Marseilles, was formed in 1996 when newly privatised CGM was sold to CMA and CMA CGM was formed. In the latest figures, its capacity is 3.1 million TEUs. One of their containers is seen on a Freightliner flat at Grangetown Junction, close to Teesport.

Based in Beijing, the China Ocean Shipping Company (COSCO) group is ranked fourth with a TEU capacity of just over 2.9 million. This COSCO container is seen in a DB Cargo working passing through Leamington Spa.

The German operator Hapaq-Lloyd is number 5 in terms of TEU rankings with a capacity of just under 1.8 million. Formed in 1970, the Hamburg-based company has completed half a century of container movements. One of their containers is seen in a DB Cargo working crossing East Anglia towards Felixstowe.

Ocean Network Express (ONE), with a TEU capacity of just under 1.6 million, is ranked number 6 container shipping operator. The Japanese operator is a recent entrant into the market following a number of company mergers, creating ONE in 2016. The company's striking magenta house colour was unveiled shortly afterwards, inspired by the cherry blossom, which is one of the national symbols of Japan. A ONE container rests on a Freightliner flat wagon in Southampton Maritime terminal in September 2020.

Evergreen Marine is ranked at number 7, with a capacity of just under 1.6 million TEUs. Evergreen, a global company based in Taiwan, also has over half a century operating in the shipping container marketplace. One of its ships, Ever Given, made the world headlines when it became stuck in the Suez Canal in March 2021. One of the company's familiar green-liveried containers is seen passing Bury St Edmunds on a GBRf working.

HMM, rebranded from Hyundai Merchant Marine in 2020, ranked number 8 with a TEU capacity of 0.8 million. At the time of rebranding the South Korean company launched two new container ships, each with a TEU of 24,000, which, at the time of writing, makes them the largest container ships in the world. An HMM Hyundai branded 20-foot container is seen on a Lawley Street to Southampton Freightliner working in August 2021.

Yang Ming is ranked number 9 in shipping operators with a TEU capacity of 0.6 million. The company, another founded in the 1970s, is based in Taiwan. It moves containers by rail across Canada through an agreement with the Canadian Pacific Railway. One of their containers is seen passing Ely on a GBRf working.

The list of major players is completed by Zim Integrated Shipping Services with a TEU capacity of just over 0.4 million. The Israeli shipping company has its base in Haifa. One of their branded containers is seen in a Freightliner working at Peterborough.

A couple of other container brands deserve a mention. First, China Shipping is a brand that has disappeared. The structure of the group of companies involved is complex, but the China Shipping brand has been dropped in favour of COSCO following a merger in 2017. Nevertheless, China Shipping containers are still seen on our rail network. Their familiar branding is seen alongside a Maersk container in this view of a Freightliner wagon at Peterborough.

Second, P & O Nedlloyd, an Anglo-Dutch shipping line, was acquired by Maersk Line back in the mid-2000s. Despite the time lag, its branded containers are still found across the rail network. This 20-foot container is seen alongside a Maersk container at Leicester.

Appreciating Customers Through Liveries and Names

The principle of freight operators celebrating partnerships with their customers is well established. For example, in 2012, GBRf marked ten years of partnership with Mediterranean Shipping Company (MSC) by rebranding No. 66709 in the company's livery. In July 2016, the loco passes Nuneaton on a Trafford Park to Felixstowe service.

The loco side incorporates an MSC vessel and the name Sorrento. The Italian town is the hometown of MSC founder and owner Gianluigi Aponte.

Back in 2007, Freightliner loco No. 66594 was named *NYK Spirit of Kyoto*. The name reflected the Kyoto Protocol, the international agreement to stabilise greenhouse gas concentrations in the atmosphere. It reflected NYK's (Nippon Yusen Kaisha) ongoing commitment to move more containers by rail using Freightliner services.

Despite being integrated into Ocean Network Express (ONE) in 2017, NYK branded containers are still seen across the UK rail network. Loco No. 66594 retains its nameplate as of late 2021.

Freightliner named No. 66534 *OOCL Express* in 2001. The Orient Overseas Container Line (OOCL) used Freightliner to haul a regular block train between Manchester and Southampton.

One of OOCL's branded containers is seen in a Freightliner destined for Felixstowe in October 2020. The company was acquired by COSCO Shipping Lines in 2018.

Probably the most distinctive Freightliner livery is that applied to No. 66587. In a complete wrapping of Ocean Network Express (ONE) livery, it passes Kings Norton, near Banbury, in July 2020.

In June 2019, the loco was unveiled in its new livery at Southampton. Ocean Network Express was established in July 2017 by the integration of three Japanese companies, 'K' Line, MOL and NYK.

At the same time, the nameplate, 'AS ONE, WE CAN', was unveiled. The black nameplate on the loco's side contrasts with ONE's striking magenta corporate colour behind.

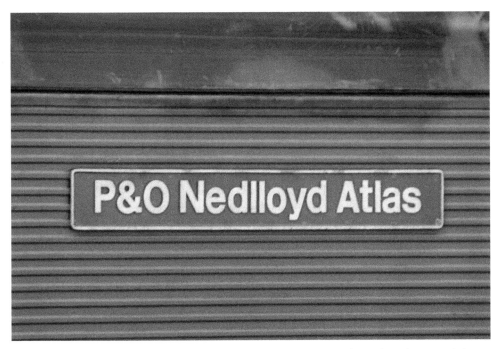

Other Freightliner loco namings in connection with the shipping industry have been much lower profile. No. 66533 was jointly named *Hanjin Express* and *Senator Express*, with one nameplate on each side of the loco, and sister loco No. 66532 named *P & O Nedlloyd Atlas*.

In 2016, GBRf unveiled Maritime livery on its loco, No. 66727, at the Birch Coppice terminal managed by Maritime. The loco is seen here passing Leicester on an intermodal to Felixstowe in August 2018.

At the same time, the loco was named *Maritime One* with the loco's 66727 numbers in large white numbering beneath.

DB Cargo's No. 66136 was chosen to be branded with Yiwu to London Train vinyls. The loco is seen on 9 February 2017 on a Burton-on-Trent to Felixstowe service through Leicester.

The branding was to mark the inaugural container run from Yiwu, eastern China, to London, which arrived via the Channel Tunnel in January 2017. The so-called Silk Road train had covered 7,500 miles in fourteen days, with the containers transferred twice between wagons during their journey.

DB Cargo selected No. 66185 for naming *DP WORLD London Gateway* in 2013. The Dubai-based company commenced work on the London Gateway port in 2010, with opening taking place in late 2013. The naming by DB Cargo coincided with the port's opening.

Freightliner loco No. 66593 was named *3MG Mersey Multimodal Gateway* in September 2008. The expanding freight complex, close to the West Coast Main Line at Ditton, Merseyside, sees regular Freightliner container services to both Felixstowe and Southampton.

DB Cargo chose their Class 66 loco, No. 66109, to receive the branding of its clients, P D Ports. In April 2019 the loco was also named *Teesport Express*, reflecting the company's long association with the north-east port. DB Cargo operate regular services from Teesport to both Mossend and Grangemouth.

DB Cargo also marked their partnership with Maritime Transport, branding No. 66005 in Maritime livery. The loco is seen at Manea on 28 April 2021 on a Wakefield Europort to Felixstowe service.

The loco was named *Maritime Intermodal One* at the Wakefield in March 2019. Sister loco No. 66047 was named *Maritime Intermodal Two* on the same day.

In a further collaboration in 2019, Maritime Intermodal took over the DB Cargo lease at Wakefield and Trafford Park in Manchester. They were followed by a similar plan for Maritime to lease the Mossend Euro Terminal, in Lanarkshire, from late 2021. In the meantime, the latest Maritime livery has been applied to DB Cargo's No. 66148 *Maritime Intermodal Seven*.

In 2019, GBRf applied a dedicated livery to their loco No. 66747, recognising their partnership with Sheffield company Newell & Wright (NWT). GBRf now operate a regular intermodal service from DP World's London Gateway to NWT's terminal at Masborough, Rotherham, alongside shipping company operator Maersk Line.

At the same time the NWT branding was applied, the loco was named *Made in Sheffield*.

In a fiercely competitive marketplace, industry partnerships come and go. In 2013, DRS Class 66 No. 66434 is seen inside their depot at Carlisle Kingmoor. At that time its Malcolm Rail livery reflected the joint venture between the two companies. Today, it has since reverted to DRS's own corporate livery.

Four years later, and the W. H. Malcolm livery is seen again. This time the loco is a DB Cargo Class 90 electric, No. 90024. It is seen in October 2017 at Carlisle on their Coatbridge to Daventry intermodal.

The Freight Operators' Wagons

A variety of wagons are in use by the container train UK operators, with Freightliner operating the majority of those wagons built before rail privatisation. This includes a small batch of flat wagons dating back to 1985, built by Standard Wagon Company in Heywood. One of these, numbered RLS92610, is seen here at Eastleigh in 2019.

A larger batch of wagons was built in 1987, in Finland, for Tiphook, one of the world's leading container wagon leasing companies at the time. Wagon TIPH93479 is seen in a Freightliner rake at Leamington Spa in 2017. Many of these Tiphook wagons remain in use today.

French wagon builders Arbel Fauvet were chosen to build one of the largest wagon orders in UK history. A total of 700 wagons, split between 140 twins and 140 triples, were in service by the end of 1993. The builder's plate on wagon 607023 is seen here.

Despite this fleet approaching thirty years in service, almost all remain in regular use with Freightliner. In 2019, 608216 is seen passing Acton Yard, West London.

The trend towards increasing container heights from 8 feet 6inches to 9 feet 6 inches left the UK rail industry with a gauging problem. Lowering the wagon's platform was considered a potential solution. This photo of pocket container wagon GERS97709, at Southampton Maritime in 2017, shows how the container nests in the centre.

A total of seventy-five of these pocket wagons were built. The prefix GERS referred to GE Rail Services, who had taken over debt-ridden Tiphook by this time. Wagon GERS97733 is seen at Didcot Parkway in 2017, loaded with a 40-foot Maersk container.

In 1991, Powell Duffryn built forty-eight low-platform wagons for Freightliner, designed to run in four- or five-wagon sets. A five-car set, with 606015 nearest the camera, is seen on the rear of a service through Water Orton.

GB Railfreight's wagon fleet includes a batch of former gypsum-carrying wagons, built in Finland in 1994, and since renumbered and reliveried for the company's container traffic. Wagon 600009, which was originally British Gypsum's BGL95319, is seen conveying an Evergreen container at Bury St Edmunds.

DB Cargo twin flat wagon 7049387257 is registered for use on Channel Tunnel workings and has been noted on one of the company's steel workings from Scunthorpe to Ebange, in France. In this photo it is on an internal UK working between Trafford Park and Southampton.

This Freightliner twin container wagon was also built by French company Arbel Fauvet. Numbered 6849430960, it is seen passing Doncaster on a service to Leeds.

One of the post-privatisation orders saw DB Cargo receive 150 twin intermodal wagons, numbered 704908000 to 704908149. These were built at Thrall Europa's workshops in York. Their wagon, numbered 7049081109, is seen passing Carlisle conveying a W. H. Malcolm container.

In common with other UK operators, Direct Rail Services has a fleet of megafret twin container wagons. They offer a modern-day answer to the UK's restrictive loading gauge. They, too, are built by French company Arbel Fauvet to carry the 9-foot 6-inch hi-cube containers. Megafret, numbered 6849096225, is seen on an Anglo-Scottish working in 2019.

GB Railfreight also has a substantial pool of these megafret twin wagons. Two Maersk containers are seen at Leicester heading for Felixstowe being carried on wagon 8049091523.

DB Cargo ordered 400 twin flat wagons in 2000, built by Thrall Europa, York, with each half of the pair individually numbered from 610001 to 610400. An MSC container rests on wagon 610101 at Leicester in 2016.

Freightliner saw delivery of another substantial fleet of twin flat wagons from 2003, numbered from 640001 to 640500. A Maersk container sits on wagon 640414 at Didcot Parkway in 2017. These wagons were built by European wagon manufacturer, Greenbrier.

Greenbrier was also responsible for building a similar batch of fifty-four wagons for GBRf around the same time, numbered 650001 to 650054, including 650028 seen here at Peterborough in 2017.

In 2004, the same manufacturer built eighty low-platform twin flats, numbered 606101 to 606180, for Freightliner. A pair of empty wagons, 606171 and 606172, is seen here at Nuneaton.

In the last few years, a container train's carrying capacity has been increased through the introduction of ecofret wagons, aimed to outstrip the megafrets. The design pioneers, VTG Rail, have used the eco prefix to stress the wagon's green credentials, as they aim to reduce the empty space between containers on wagons. A well loaded Freightliner pairing of 7045200388 and 7045200396 is seen passing Eastleigh.

GBRf are operating these ecofrets as triple sets. Their newly delivered wagon, 7045202491, is seen at the rear of a working through Peterborough in June 2021.

The next generation of Freightliner wagons started to arrive in the UK in September 2021. These Greenbrier-built wagons are 2 tonnes lighter than similar wagons currently in use and also benefit from each wagon being more closely coupled. The freight operator claims the features on wagons like 7048460809, seen here at Nuneaton, will reduce carbon emissions by a further 7 per cent.

One of Freightliner's main maintenance hubs for servicing and repairs to their wagon fleet, as well as some loco work, is at Southampton Maritime. This is a busy scene in September 2020 with the depot's diesel shunters, 08585 and 08785, present along with other locos and wagons.

The steady growth of GBRf's freight business has necessitated bringing wagons from Europe to the UK, including French registered intermodal flats. Recent arrival, wagon number 8749060012, is seen in a consist passing Leicester.

Another French registered wagon, 8749093872, is seen at Ely on the rear of a Doncaster to Felixstowe intermodal in May 2021.

Tanktainers and Binliners

Throughout this publication we have concentrated on shipping containers moving by rail in the UK. Some container variants are worthy of mention, such as the tank container, or 'tanktainer'. These can carry liquids, gases or powders. An example is seen on the rear of this working through Ipswich in 2016, carried on wagon RLS92613.

With a UK base at Romford in Essex, Stolt Tank Containers is a global provider of logistics, maintenance and management services for door-to-door shipment of bulk liquid chemicals and food grade products. Their containers are in the consist of Freightliner's Cardiff Wentloog to Southampton service.

EXSIF is one of the world's leading tanktainer leasing companies, claiming an available fleet of over 60,000 tanks. One of their tanks, carrying ethyl acetate, is seen on DB Cargo's wagon 610341 at Peterborough in 2018.

Any loading on the southbound empty Tesco working from Inverness to Mossend is a bonus. A Scotland Gas tanktainer is seen on the rear of this working passing Blair Atholl. The DRS wagon is numbered 6849096621.

A variety of other containers can be found on domestic services within the UK. Notably, a number of block trains moving household waste for landfill or burning can be seen across the network. On 13 May 2013, Freightliner's No. 66553 heads north through Doncaster on one such 'binliner' working.

This Freightliner working ran for a number of years, moving containers on behalf of Greater Manchester Waste Disposal Authority, in partnership with Viridor. The jointly branded container, on wagon GMC92502, is heading for the disused iron ore quarry at Roxby Gullet, near Scunthorpe.

Freightliner recognised the importance of this traffic by the naming of their loco, No. 66597, *Viridor* in 2011.

Freightliner went one stage further in their collaboration with waste management company Shanks & McKewan. Half of their loco, No. 66522, was rebranded in Shanks' house colours between 2004 and 2018. The loco is seen passing Nuneaton on a container working shortly before the branding was removed.

DB Cargo also handle binliner traffic at various locations. Since 2016, this has included the flow from Knowsley on Merseyside to Wilton on Teesside. Liverpool's waste is burned at a newly built 'Energy from Waste' (EfW) power station there. On 29 September 2021, No. 66105 passes Salford Crescent on the returning empties to Knowsley.

One of the DB Cargo wagons used on these services, 610258, is seen, complete with containers, in the wagon repair area at Tees Yard.

DB Cargo has operated a number of binliner container workings to the waste transfer station at the landfill site at Calvert, Buckinghamshire. Their wagon, 610320, is seen at West Hampstead whilst the train loco runs round its train to Calvert.

Another EfW power station, served by rail, is at the former ICI works at Severnside near Bristol. Waste for burning is transported there from Northolt and Brentford. On 16 June 2021, a loaded service heads westbound through Reading, hauled by No. 66061.

DB Cargo's 610052 is seen on the rear of this working to Severnside, with an older branding on its containers.

The more distinctive blue livery is now a familiar sight on the Great Western Main Line, as seen on wagon 610334. Suez Recovery operate the Severnside site which receives household waste from 1.6 million homes in a number of London boroughs.

Despite their use of open wagons rather than containers, it is worth including a mention of the collaboration between Biffa and GBRf. The two companies have joined forces, handling waste from a rail served terminal at Renwick Road in Barking. The colourful colours of Biffa have been applied to GBRf's No. 66783. It is seen at Doncaster on its way to its nameplate unveiling as The Flying Dustman.